Rosa and the Runaway Ram

Contents

A City Girl in the Countryside	3
A Rampage in the City	31

Written by Gareth Osborne
Illustrated by Nina de Polonia

Published by Pearson Education Limited, Edinburgh Gate, Harlow, Essex, CM20 2JE.

www.pearsonschools.co.uk

Text © Gareth Osborne 2013

Designed by Bigtop
Original illustrations © Pearson Education 2013
Illustrated by Nina de Polonia, Advocate Art

The right of Gareth Osborne to be identified as author of this work has been asserted by him in accordance with the Copyright, Designs and Patents Act 1988.

First published 2013

17 16 15 14 13
10 9 8 7 6 5 4 3 2 1

British Library Cataloguing in Publication Data
A catalogue record for this book is available from the British Library

ISBN 978 0 435 14376 3

Copyright notice
All rights reserved. No part of this publication may be reproduced in any form or by any means (including photocopying or storing it in any medium by electronic means and whether or not transiently or incidentally to some other use of this publication) without the written permission of the copyright owner, except in accordance with the provisions of the Copyright, Designs and Patents Act 1988 or under the terms of a licence issued by the Copyright Licensing Agency, Saffron House, 6–10 Kirby Street, London EC1N 8TS (www.cla.co.uk). Applications for the copyright owner's written permission should be addressed to the publisher.

Printed in Malaysia (CTP-PPSB)

Acknowledgements
We would like to thank Bangor Central Integrated Primary School, Northern Ireland; Bishop Henderson Church of England Primary School, Somerset; Bletchingdon Parochial Church of England Primary School, Oxfordshire; Brookside Community Primary School, Somerset; Bude Park Primary School, Hull; Cheddington Combined School, Buckinghamshire; Dair House Independent School, Buckinghamshire; Glebe Infant School, Gloucestershire; Henley Green Primary School, Coventry; Lovelace Primary School, Surrey; Our Lady of Peace Junior School, Slough; Tackley Church of England Primary School, Oxfordshire; and Twyford Church of England School, Buckinghamshire for their invaluable help in the development and trialling of the Bug Club resources.

Every effort has been made to contact copyright holders of material reproduced in this book. Any omissions will be rectified in subsequent printings if notice is given to the publishers.

A City Girl in the Countryside

Chapter One

Señorita Rosa Fernández García winced as the flat doorbell rang. It was eight o'clock on a Friday evening. She didn't want any unplanned developments so close to the weekend she'd been looking forward to all month.

Rosa lived in Madrid, the capital of Spain, and she was a city girl through and through. There was nothing she liked more than smart clothes and shiny shoes. This weekend Rosa and her friends had tickets to a local fashion show, and afterwards her friend's mother was taking them for iced *horchatas* – tigernut milkshakes – on a sunny café terrace near the park.

She quickly finished dressing and pressed an ear to her bedroom door. Outside in the hall she heard her mother answer the intercom. A deep, cheerful voice sounded back through the handset. Rosa winced again. What she didn't like so much were surprise visits from her grandfather on one of his rare trips to the city. That voice could only be his.

Her grandfather lived in a mountain village called Cantagallo, which roughly translates as 'Crowing Cockerel'. It wasn't that Rosa didn't like Grandpa Paco. She loved him, of course she did. She just didn't like how he always smelled of old leather and stale sheep, and how the dirt under his finger-nails stained her dresses when he hugged her.

Grandpa Paco was a shepherd, one of the last in the country he always said. Rosa used to go to Cantagallo to visit him every other weekend when she was younger, but recently she'd been so busy with her friends, she just hadn't had the time. She was ten years old now anyway, far too grown up to be hanging around on a farm looking after lambs. How on earth could she explain to her city-girl friends that she was going to miss one of their weekend gossiping sessions to go and muck out filthy, smelly sheep pens in the countryside?

"Rosa!" her mother called a few minutes later. "Will you come through to the living room, please? Grandpa Paco's got some surprises for you."

"Coming *Mamá*!" Rosa replied, grimacing. *Surprises? More than one of them?*

As always, Grandpa Paco sat down on the best sofa in the lounge and started handing out presents from an old potato sack. He gave Rosa a doll that he'd fashioned for her out of straw, and a huge wedge of his best cave-matured cheese.

Her mother made her kiss Grandpa Paco's bristly, sheepy cheek even though she didn't play with dolls anymore and didn't like cheese either; at least not the kind that looked as though it was about three hundred years past its use-by date.

"You know, *bonita*," Grandpa Paco said, "I shouldn't really be the one giving out presents at all."

"Why's that, Grandpa?" asked Rosa, hoping that they'd finished with the surprises for this visit.

"I should be the one *getting* them! This weekend it's my birthday. Eighty-five years old, I'll be! Can you imagine that?"

Rosa definitely couldn't imagine that, not even by adding up the ages of all her friends and multiplying by two.

"Now, if I may, I'd like to ask your mother something – *in private*," said Grandpa Paco, winking at her as he guided her mother out of the room.

Rosa didn't like being winked at. In her experience it always meant that something unexpected was about to happen. While she waited on the sofa, sipping a *horchata*, she had the sinking feeling that another surprise was being prepared.

Her mother came back through alone.

"Grandpa Paco has decided what he wants for his birthday," she said.

"And what's that then?" asked Rosa, in a slightly squeaky voice.

"*You*," said her mother, smiling.

"*Me?*" exclaimed Rosa. "But ..." She drew her lips into a tight line. "Well, he can't have me. I'm mine. I belong to myself."

"Don't worry," said her mother. "He only wants you for his birthday, this weekend – to go and stay with him on his farm like you used to. Of course you can have yourself back afterwards."

"But *Mamá*," Rosa pleaded. "We've got tickets to ..."

"But nothing," her mum said quickly. "I've already said you'll go."

Rosa's shoulders slumped in resignation.

Chapter Two

The next morning, Rosa contacted all her friends to tell them that she'd be away for the weekend, so they should go ahead with their plans without her. Then she started packing her suitcase to go to Grandpa Paco's farm.

During the short journey on the air-conditioned train, Rosa pondered the two days that were to come. *All I have to do,* she thought, *is make sure Grandpa Paco has a lovely birthday and then I'll never have to go back to 'Crowing Cockerel' ever again.*

When Rosa arrived, Grandpa Paco took her on a walk around the farm. Rosa soon realised that something rather important was missing.

"Where are all the sheep, Grandpa?" she asked, frowning. "I remember there were millions of them all over the place last time I visited."

Grandpa Paco laughed. "Not quite millions. But hundreds, yes. They're all still grazing in the mountains to the north. There's a month to go before we have to drive the sheep down to their winter grazing fields south of the city."

Rosa couldn't believe her luck. *No smelly sheep!* she thought with glee, while making sure she looked as sad as possible for Grandpa Paco. Maybe these two days weren't going to be so bad after all. She'd be back in Madrid before she knew it, without so much as a splatter of mud on any of her lovely dresses …

Grandpa Paco sighed. "Okay, okay. Tomorrow's my birthday and I *had* planned a picnic in my vineyard for the two of us," he said, "but seeing as you look so disappointed, here's what we can do.

Tomorrow we'll take the donkeys up the mountain pass and go and see the sheep instead. How does that sound?"

Rosa wanted to say that a long, bumpy donkey ride to see a huge flock of sheep didn't suit her at all, and that sitting in a cool, shady vineyard really sounded quite nice, but Grandpa Paco had already nodded firmly as though his mind was made up.

Before the next morning arrived, there were more countryside ordeals to survive – more than a city girl should ever be put through.

It started with dinner, which was nice enough, except that they ate in a cellar beneath the house where Grandpa Paco kept his wine barrels and cheese – *in a cellar, of all places!*

"It's lovely and cool down here, isn't it?" Grandpa Paco said, obviously thrilled with his idea.

"It's certainly not hot," said Rosa politely and pulled her dress down around her shivering knees.

Then there were the crickets chirruping in the evening, and the dogs making a hullabaloo at night, and the smoke from the chimney that seemed to get absolutely everywhere – in her dresses, in her suitcase, *even under her bed covers!*

By the time morning came, Rosa felt and looked like a grumpy old ewe.

"Your long wait is finally over, *mi pequeñita*," said Grandpa Paco theatrically once they'd cleared away the breakfast things. His eyes were glittering with a dangerous enthusiasm. "Now we can finally go and see those beloved sheep of yours."

Rosa's smile flickered, but didn't fall. It was Grandpa Paco's birthday after all; that was the important thing. And anyway, she had the feeling the worst of the countryside was already over ...

Chapter Three

Rosa's donkey was a shaggy, flea-bitten thing called Leopoldo.

Leopoldo must have liked city girls a bit too much, because along the path to the mountains he bent his head around every two minutes to nibble on Rosa's toes, bucking with glee whenever he got one.

But toes were the least of Rosa's problems. Her bottom was soon so sore from being bumped up and down on Leopoldo's saddle that she couldn't have sat on a nice shady café terrace with her friends if her life had depended on it.

After what seemed like miles of riding, Grandpa Paco suddenly shouted, "There they are!" and galloped off towards the sea of woolly backs, stained with mud and other un-nameable things, that was filling the path ahead.

"Stay, Leopoldo! Stay!" Rosa hissed into the donkey's tufty ear, but sheep were obviously Leopoldo's second favourite thing in the world, after city girls' toes. With a loud "eeyore" that sent donkey drool spraying into the air, he plunged into the middle of the flock of sheep.

Rosa tried to keep her feet up in the air away from all the munching heads and held her silk handkerchief to her face. She had to keep out the terrible smell that was wafting up from them, making her eyes water.

Grandpa Paco smiled when he noticed her tears. "Don't be upset, Rosa, *mi amor*. I know how much you've missed your sheep. They're beautiful, aren't they?"

Rosa didn't have the chance to reply, for a worried expression suddenly fell over her grandfather's face. He deftly hooked one of the passing sheep with his shepherd's crook, and manoeuvred it quickly around to see behind it. Then he gritted his teeth and looked out over the fields.

"What's the matter, Grandpa?" asked Rosa quietly.

"This ewe always has her lamb with her, a young black-faced ram with white ears, but I can't see him anywhere." Grandpa Paco shook his head and muttered, "He's always getting himself into trouble, is that one."

Grandpa Paco guided his donkey off the path, scanning the horizon intently. Rosa spurred Leopoldo on after him.

They searched for the young ram amongst the rocky outcrops that dotted the steep mountain field and behind any bush or tree they passed, but there was no sign of him anywhere.

Then as they neared the top of the field, Rosa pulled Leopoldo to a halt and listened. "*I think I can hear him, Grandpa,*" she hissed.

"There he is!" said Grandpa Paco, pointing ahead towards the corner of the field.

Rosa grimaced as she saw what had happened. The young ram had obviously tried to jump a low stone wall and had become ensnared in the barbed wire above it. The more he bucked and wriggled to free himself, the more the barbed wire tightened and bit into his hind legs.

The young ram bleated loudly as Grandpa Paco strode over the muddy ground towards him.

"We've got to get that wire off quickly," said Rosa, jumping down from her donkey into the mud and running to her grandfather's side.

"You take his head then," said Grandpa Paco. "Try to soothe him while I get to work on his legs."

Rosa stared at the young ram for a second and swallowed hard. *Could* she touch him?

23

She gritted her teeth, walked forward and gripped the young ram's head under her arm. His eyes flared wildly at her. "Don't worry, *pequeñín*," she said softly. "It'll all be over soon." She hesitated for a moment, then began to stroke his furry black face with her free hand. Apart from an occasional grunt of pain, he seemed to calm in her arms.

"There," said Grandpa Paco a few minutes later. "All done. The wire's off and I've cleaned the wounds. He should be as right as rain in a couple of days."

Rosa let go of the young ram, but for a moment he seemed to stay there in her lap, looking up at her in thanks. Then he leaped up and butted her hard in the chest before capering lamely back down to the flock again.

"Ungrateful rascal!" Grandpa Paco shouted after him.

"It's okay," said Rosa quickly. "It means he can't be hurt too badly."

Grandpa Paco smiled at her strangely.

"What's the matter?" asked Rosa, shooting him a confused glance.

"Nothing, nothing," he replied. "I was just looking at that nice, prim dress of yours."

Rosa looked down. Her dress was so covered with mud that not a single flower of the pattern showed through. With everything that had happened, she hadn't noticed how dirty she was getting.

"That's the way it's always been," said her grandfather. "When your flock's in danger, nothing else is important. I remember when we shepherds used to be allowed to drive our sheep all over Spain. Back then, wolves were the danger you had to look out for the most …"

Chapter Four

Grandpa Paco was still talking about sheep herding when they arrived at the station later that evening.

"My train's here, Grandpa," Rosa interrupted politely, as it screeched to a halt in front of them. If she hurried, she'd be back in the city in time to catch a last glimpse of the fashion show. She hadn't minded missing it so much in the end. The sound of the young ram bleating happily by its mother's side echoed in her ears. There were more important things in life, after all, she thought.

Rosa climbed up into the carriage.

"I just wanted to thank you, Rosa," said Grandpa Paco, coming to the door. "It's been the best birthday I've ever had."

Rosa suddenly realised just how much she was going to miss him. She couldn't help leaping down onto the platform to give him one last sheepy hug. Her stay in the countryside hadn't been so bad after all. Despite the smoke and the insects and the mud and the toe-nibbling, it had even been fun in parts.

She was sure she'd never be able to explain that to her friends back in the city though. They were from a different world to Grandpa Paco. Just as well really, she thought, chuckling to herself as the train pulled away. She couldn't imagine what would happen if they ever came together.

A Rampage in the City

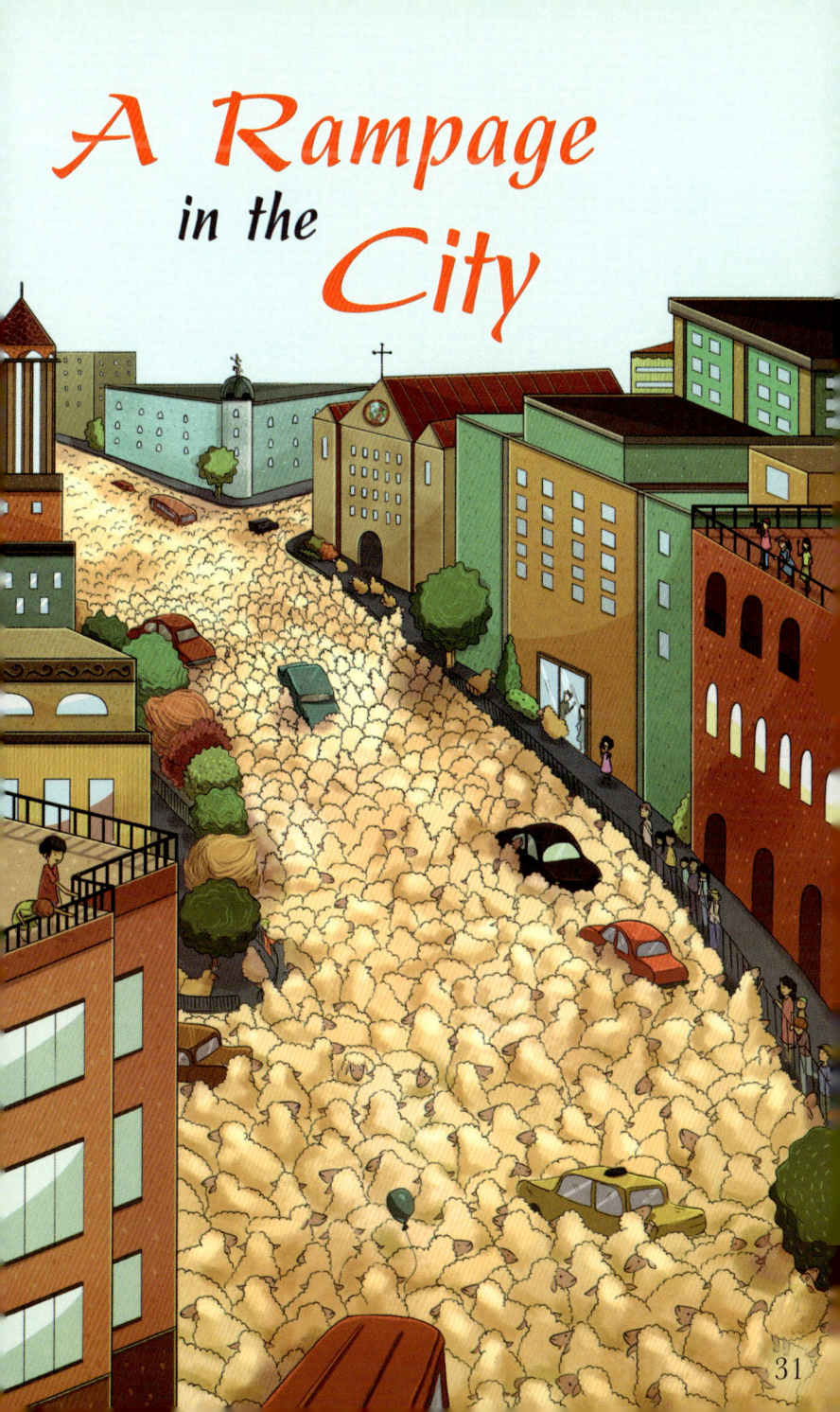

31

Chapter One

"It is a shame, isn't it, *Mamá*?" said Señorita Rosa Fernández García. She was standing atop a stool in front of the mirror, in *La Bella Conchita* boutique on Madrid's fashionable Goya Street.

"What did you say, *cariño*?" asked her mother, looking at dresses nearby.

"I said, it's a shame Grandpa Paco doesn't come to the city more often to visit us," said Rosa.

"Why on earth wouldn't he come to visit such a pretty little granddaughter as you?" came a high-pitched voice from behind them. It was Olivia, the glamorous shop assistant that Rosa admired so much.

Rosa's face turned a deep scarlet. She hadn't realised Olivia had been listening. "Because he's a shepherd, that's why," said Rosa, as proudly as she could, "in a little village called Cantagallo."

"*Crowing Cockerel!*" Olivia's eyes widened, as if she were imagining exactly how rural and rustic a village with such a name would be.

"Yes," said Rosa. "It's in the mountains, north of Madrid."

"I'll have to take your word for it, I'm afraid," said Olivia. "I don't go up mountains. There are goats and other such hairy things up mountains."

As the shop assistant drifted back to her work, Rosa's mother turned to Rosa and whispered, "I forgot to tell you. Grandpa Paco *is* coming to the city next week."

"*Really?*" Rosa asked, excitedly.

"Yes, he's bringing his sheep."

Rosa frowned, suddenly less excited. "*Bringing his sheep?* To the city? Why would he do that?"

"Winter's coming and the sheep need to be moved to the warmer fields in the south," said her mother. "Shepherds are still allowed to herd their sheep through the city centre once a year. Don't you remember last year? They blocked off the roads and everything."

"Sounds like a terrible lot of smelly old work to me," said Rosa. She had forgotten all about the annual sheep drive, and her nose began to twitch at the thought.

"I said you'd give him a hand this year," added her mother casually.

"*You said what?!*" Rosa stared at her mother in disbelief.

"Grandpa Paco's eighty-five now, Rosa. He plans to retire from shepherding next year. It's going to be his last sheep drive ever. Isn't that something special you'd like to share with him?"

"I guess so," Rosa admitted.

"He said it would make him the happiest old shepherd in the country if you accompanied him on this last one," her mother continued. "For the leg through the city at least."

On the way home, Rosa nervously contemplated the disaster she'd failed to wriggle her way out of. She, *Rosa Fernández García*, herd a flock of a sheep through the streets of her beloved Madrid? What if her friends saw her? It just didn't bear thinking about.

Chapter Two

It was a five-day walk at a sheep's pace from Cantagallo in the mountains northwest of Madrid to the winter fields to the south. Thankfully, Rosa had negotiated with her mother to accompany Grandpa Paco and his herd just for the six-hour leg through the city.

Grandpa Paco was waiting for her at the bus stop in Brunete, the last village in the countryside before they entered Madrid. When he saw Rosa, he put his sweaty old flat cap on her head and hugged her until she couldn't breathe. "You're going to be the best shepherdess this country has ever seen, *Rosita mía*," he said.

As they walked to pick up his herd again, Rosa tried one last time to avoid the humiliation she seemed destined for. "Can't we take the sheep around the city, Grandpa?" she asked. "It just seems such a bother to drive them through the centre, doesn't it?"

Grandpa Paco's bushy eyebrows twitched with a passion she'd never seen in them before. "It's the way it's always been done, Rosa. Your great-grandfather, and his father, and his father before him, all drove their flocks along this route to the winter fields. Just because they went and built a city in the way, does that mean we have to give up our ancient tradition?"

It was an ancient tradition that Rosa wasn't sure she agreed with. Where, for example, were all these dirty beasts going to do their business while they were in the streets of her lovely city? She didn't raise this last point though, as Grandpa Paco was staring grimly out over the fields at the distant skyscrapers of the city, like an army general planning a grand invasion.

Rosa could already see her grandfather's sheep milling about in the village square at the end of the road, rubbing their heads on lampposts, chewing the corners of benches, and nibbling on the flower boxes of the village hall.

Grandpa Paco handed her a long wooden shepherd's crook and a pile of clothes – a shirt, some trousers, a waistcoat, a neck scarf, and a flat cap.

Rosa begged for mercy with her eyes.

"What's wrong with them?" asked Grandpa Paco, gesturing at his own identical outfit.

"Can't I wear what I'm already wearing?" she asked.

"Shepherdesses don't wear flowery dresses, I'm afraid. The sheep would just think it's dinnertime and be nibbling round your hem all the time!"

Rosa's eyes widened in horror and she hastily put on the shepherding clothes. They were itchy and made her feel like flexing her muscles. She wasn't sure she liked the feeling.

41

Chapter Three

There was no neat cutting of a ribbon to signal the start of the next leg of the sheep drive. The flock just suddenly started to flow out of the village square and down the street towards them, like a living wave of wool with a hundred yellow eyes.

Rosa got behind her grandfather as his sheep clattered past them on all sides. The sheepy smell in the narrow village streets was unbearable.

When the sheep had passed, Grandpa Paco started walking after them. Rosa followed, holding onto his big rough hand. The village gave way to the countryside and a warm breeze that smelt of rosemary and pine blew softly into Rosa's face.

Surrounded by the peaceful baaing of the sheep, she felt a calmness settle over her. For once, there were no friends to rush off and meet, and no after-school activities to get ready for. She found she was thinking of nothing at all, and the nothingness was strangely delicious.

Then they arrived in the city.

They merged with other shepherds bringing their flocks from the north. Together, they formed one bleating river of sheep, three thousand strong, that poured through the streets of the capital. From the very first neighbourhoods they passed through, the pavements were lined with people, all cheering them on, all looking them up and down as though they were walking exhibits in a farming museum. Rosa pulled her scarf up over her face and hoped that nobody would recognise her.

Soon they arrived in Barrio Salamanca, the most elegant and fashionable area of the city – Rosa's neighbourhood. She bowed her head as she passed her friends' apartments. They probably wouldn't be watching anyway, she told herself. They'd be on a sunny café terrace somewhere, sipping cool, refreshing drinks.

Suddenly Rosa heard a voice, "*Hola!* Rooosssaaa! Over here! It's Esmeralda and Marisol! We've come to watch you!"

Rosa nearly swallowed her scarf in shock. *How had* they *found out?* She'd sworn her mother to complete and utter secrecy. In a panic, Rosa hunched her back, limped a little, and ignored her friends' shouts altogether. Maybe they'd think they were mistaken and that she wasn't who they thought she was at all.

But with one disaster narrowly averted, as they were passing the city park, *another* struck.

Chapter Four

Outside the park gates, an adult ram suddenly broke away from her grandfather's flock and charged into the crowds. The people on the pavement screamed and scattered away from the bad-tempered animal as it butted handbags and bottoms as though it was having the time of its life.

Rosa turned to where Grandpa Paco had been standing beside her, but he wasn't there any more. She spotted him twenty metres away, sprinting in giant strides across the road towards the commotion.

As quick as a flash, he hooked the ram's back leg with his crook. Then he grabbed its horns and lifted the hefty animal up off the floor, carrying it back to the flock under his arm. The ram kicked and bucked and squirmed and butted, but her grandfather's thick brown arm held it fast. He placed it back on the ground and, with a slap on its rump, it disappeared into the flock again, abashed and defeated.

Rosa stood with her mouth open. She'd never seen anybody do anything like that before. She'd never thought Grandpa Paco was so quick and strong and skilful. The crowd on the pavement thought so too and cheered him so loudly for his daring feat that he was eventually forced to hold his hand up to thank them all. Rosa lowered the scarf from her face and a warm feeling of pride surged through her.

That was *her* grandfather that everyone was cheering.

Her thoughts were interrupted by a distant bleating coming from somewhere behind her. She turned just in time to see a woolly rump bobbing away down a nearby alley. It belonged to another sheep from her grandfather's flock, a young ram that was obviously trying to use the chaos as cover for a getaway of its own.

Rosa opened her mouth to call to Grandpa Paco, but he was too far away. He'd never hear her. She looked back at the young ram. If she went to fetch Grandpa Paco, she would lose sight of it, and she knew how devastated he'd be if he was the only shepherd on the sheep drive to lose an animal from his flock. She narrowed her eyes and tightened her grip on her crook. It was all down to her now.

The young ram paused to munch on the contents of a plant pot, obviously enjoying its new-found freedom. As it turned, Rosa saw its black face and white ears. It was the same young ram that she'd rescued on her last visit to her grandfather's village! She swallowed hard as she remembered just how mischievous it had been then too, and moved towards the ram. But before she could reach the ram, with a little jump of joy, it disappeared through a doorway in the alley wall.

Rosa hurried after the troublesome ram, an uneasy feeling building in her stomach. *Why was this doorway so familiar? Where was this alley exactly?* Then she realised. She was directly behind Goya Street. This doorway led straight into the back of ... *La Bella Conchita*, her favourite clothing boutique ever. Rosa took a deep breath, pulled her shepherdess's cap down over her face and crept in through the doorway.

She came out in the ladies' changing rooms at the back of the boutique. Rosa saw the curtain tremble on the last cubicle on the left. Some rather excited bleating came from inside. She tip-toed down the aisle towards it.

As she neared the cubicle, four hairy legs flashed briefly into view beneath the curtain. Rosa gritted her teeth, whipped her shepherdess's crook through the air, and hooked it just above the hoof. She grinned at her success, but the young ram was surprisingly strong and jerked her forwards into the cubicle with it. Rosa and the young ram stared at each other for a few seconds, each as shocked as the other. Then Rosa grabbed the young ram's horns, trying to remember exactly how her grandfather had done it just moments before.

The young ram was having none of it and butted her in the chest, pinning her up against the wall. Somebody in the next cubicle complained about the noise. Rosa apologised as loudly as she could while she struggled with the bucking animal until she had both hands round its neck and was hugging it with her face pressed into its woolly back. Then her hands found its front legs and heaving with all her might, she lifted them off the floor.

For a moment they circled and spun together in the strangest of strange waltzes, but now that the young ram had only two feet on the floor and not four, Rosa found she could direct it quite easily. The young ram bleated in protest but could do nothing as she walked it out of the cubicle on its back legs and off towards the door again.

"And just where do you think you're going with that woolly jumper?!" A stern voice came from behind her.

Rosa turned and realised with horror that it was Olivia, the shop assistant with the amazing dress sense that Rosa aspired to so much.

Rosa held the young ram up to hide her face.

The shop assistant jumped backwards as what she had thought was a woolly jumper bleated at her. Then she squinted at Rosa through the young ram's horns and said, "Wait a minute. Aren't you that pretty young girl who comes in here sometimes with her mother?"

Realising her cover was blown, Rosa held her head up high and turned her ram towards the door again. "I might be," she said over her shoulder. Then she marched the young ram out into the street again, leaving the shop assistant staring after her with her mouth open.

When Rosa came out of the alley into the street, Grandpa Paco saw her immediately and came running over. His eyes widened when he saw the young ram, and widened even further when she explained what had happened. He laughed a little bit too loudly at her new shepherding waltz-technique, but even so she let him swing her up into the air and pronounce her the best shepherdess the world had ever seen.

"Rooosssaaa! Rooosssaaaa!" two voices sang out in unison from behind them.

Rosa froze. Her friends had finally cornered her. The sheep was now out of the bag.

To her surprise, she saw that her two friends were standing across the street, whistling and clapping even more loudly than everybody else. "You go, girl!" they shouted, giving her a thumbs up sign.

Rosa's heart swelled with pride again and suddenly it struck her as sad that Grandpa Paco would never go on another sheep drive again in all his life. She decided then and there that she'd go to visit him in Cantagallo more often. She wanted to hear all the stories of the other sheep drives he'd been on. And maybe, just maybe – if there were no city-girl things to do, of course – she might go on one by herself some day.